Wearable Technology

The Future of Fashion and Function

Neil King

Introduction

Importance of Wearable Technology

Wearable technology has been around for a while now, but it is only in recent years that it has become a mainstream phenomenon. The rise of smartwatches and fitness trackers has made wearable technology more accessible to the masses, and it is now an integral part of our lives. From smart glasses to smart clothing, the possibilities of wearable technology are endless.

One of the key advantages of wearable technology is its ability to collect data. Wearable devices can collect data on a range of metrics such as heart rate, blood pressure, and steps taken. This data can then be used to monitor our health and fitness levels, allowing us to make informed decisions about our lifestyles. Wearable technology can also be used to monitor the health of patients, making healthcare more efficient and effective.

Another advantage of wearable technology is its ability to enhance our experiences. Virtual and augmented reality technologies are being used to create immersive experiences in gaming, entertainment, and education. Wearable technology can also be used to create personalized experiences, such as customized workouts or personalized shopping experiences.

The Internet of Things (IoT) is also a key area where wearable technology is making a big impact. Wearable devices can be connected to other IoT devices, such as smart home systems, to create a seamless experience. This technology can be used to automate tasks, such as turning on lights or adjusting the temperature, making our lives easier and more efficient.

However, with the benefits of wearable technology come the concerns of cybersecurity and data privacy. As wearable devices collect personal data, it is important to ensure that this data is kept secure and private. Companies need to be transparent about how they collect and use data, and individuals need to be aware of the risks and take steps to protect their data.

Artificial intelligence and machine learning are also playing a big role in the development of wearable technology. These technologies are being used to create more intelligent and intuitive devices, which can adapt to the user's needs and preferences. 3D printing and additive manufacturing are also being used to create custom-fit wearable devices, making them more comfortable and practical to use.

In conclusion, wearable technology is an important area of development for the future of technology and business. It has the potential to enhance our lives in many ways, from monitoring our health to creating immersive experiences. However, it is important to address the concerns of cybersecurity and data privacy, and to ensure that wearable devices are developed with the user's needs in mind.

Brief History of Wearable Technology

The history of wearable technology dates back to the 17th century when pocket watches were invented. However, it was not until the 20th century that wearable technology began to take shape. The first wearable computer was invented in 1961 by Edward O. Thorp, a mathematician who created a device to predict the outcome of roulette. The device was strapped to his body and used to calculate the speed of the ball and wheel.

The 1980s saw the rise of digital watches and personal music players like the Sony Walkman. These devices were portable and could be worn on the body, making them the earliest forms of wearable technology. In the 1990s, the first wearable fitness trackers were introduced, paving the way for the current trend of health-focused wearables.

The 21st century has brought about a new era of wearable technology, starting with the introduction of the Bluetooth headset in 2000. The first smartwatch, the Fossil Wrist PDA, was introduced in 2003, followed by the Apple Watch in 2015. Smartwatches have since become a popular form of wearable technology, offering features such as fitness tracking, mobile payments, and even voice assistants.

Other forms of wearable technology include smart glasses, known as augmented reality (AR) glasses, which offer a virtual overlay of information on the real world. Virtual reality (VR) headsets have also become popular, offering immersive experiences in gaming, education, and even therapy.

The Internet of Things (IoT) has also played a role in the development of wearable technology. IoT devices such as smart clothing and jewelry provide data on the wearer's health and environment, making it easier to track and manage health and wellness goals.

As wearable technology becomes more prevalent, concerns about cybersecurity and data privacy have also emerged. Companies are working to ensure that wearable devices are secure and have proper privacy controls to protect users' data.

Artificial intelligence (AI) and machine learning have also been integrated into wearable technology, allowing devices to learn and adapt to the wearer's preferences and behavior.

Finally, 3D printing and additive manufacturing have made it possible for wearable technology to be customized and personalized for each individual user.

In conclusion, wearable technology has come a long way since the invention of the pocket watch. As technology continues to advance, we can expect to see even more innovative and functional wearables in the future.

Key Advancements in Wearable Technology

Wearable technology is rapidly advancing in today's world. The fusion of fashion and function has revolutionized the way we interact with technology. Today, wearable technology is more than just a fashion accessory, it is a necessity. Here are some of the key advancements in wearable technology that have contributed to its growth and popularity:

1. Health and Fitness Tracking

One of the most popular applications of wearable technology is in health and fitness tracking. Wearable devices such as Fitbit, Apple Watch, and Garmin have made it easy to monitor physical activity, heart rate, sleep patterns, and other vital signs. This technology has revolutionized the way we approach fitness and health management.

2. Virtual and Augmented Reality

Virtual and augmented reality technology is taking the world by storm. Wearable devices such as Oculus Rift, Microsoft HoloLens, and Google Glass have opened up new ways to experience virtual and augmented reality. From gaming to education, these devices have the power to change the way we live and work.

3. Internet of Things (IoT)

The Internet of Things (IoT) is a network of interconnected devices that communicate and exchange data with each other. Wearable devices play a vital role in this network. From smartwatches to fitness trackers, wearable devices are constantly collecting data and transmitting it to other devices. This technology has the potential to revolutionize industries such as healthcare, transportation, and manufacturing.

4. Cybersecurity and Data Privacy

With the growth of wearable technology, cybersecurity and data privacy have become major concerns. Companies that manufacture wearable devices must ensure that their products are secure and protect user data. Features such as two-factor authentication, encryption, and biometric authentication are becoming increasingly important.

5. Artificial Intelligence and Machine Learning

Artificial intelligence (AI) and machine learning are transforming the way we interact with technology. Wearable devices such as smartwatches and fitness trackers are becoming more intelligent, learning from user behavior to provide personalized recommendations and insights. This technology has the potential to revolutionize industries such as healthcare, finance, and retail.

6. 3D Printing and Additive Manufacturing

3D printing and additive manufacturing are revolutionizing the way we produce goods. Wearable technology is no exception. From custom-fit prosthetics to 3D-printed jewelry, this technology is changing the way we think about design and production.

In conclusion, wearable technology is a rapidly advancing field that has the potential to change the world. From health and fitness tracking to virtual and augmented reality, this technology is revolutionizing the way we interact with the world around us. As the technology continues to evolve, we can expect to see even more exciting advancements in the future.

Overview of the Book

The book "Wearable Technology: The Future of Fashion and Function" is an in-depth exploration of the revolutionary changes the world has witnessed in the field of technology, specifically, wearable technology. The book is aimed at a trade audience interested in technology and business and the future of the world, with specific niches in technology, wearable technology, virtual and augmented reality, internet of things (IoT), cybersecurity and data privacy, artificial intelligence and machine learning, and 3D printing and additive manufacturing.

The book begins with an overview of the history of wearable technology, tracing its roots to the earliest forms of human adornment and exploring the evolution of wearable technology into the present day. It then moves on to discuss the various types of wearable technology currently available, including smartwatches, fitness trackers, smart glasses, and smart clothing, among others.

The book also delves into the potential of wearable technology to revolutionize various industries, such as healthcare, fitness, and fashion. It explores the benefits of wearable technology, including improved health outcomes, increased productivity, and enhanced customer experiences.

In addition, the book examines the challenges associated with wearable technology, including data privacy and cybersecurity concerns, and the need for effective regulation and ethical considerations. The book explores the ethical implications of wearable technology, including the potential for discrimination and the impact on individual privacy.

Finally, the book concludes with a discussion of the future of wearable technology, predicting the continued growth and expansion of the industry, and exploring the potential for new technologies such as virtual and augmented reality, artificial intelligence and machine learning, and 3D printing and additive manufacturing to transform the field.

Overall, "Wearable Technology: The Future of Fashion and Function" is an essential read for anyone interested in the intersection of technology and fashion, and the ways in which wearable technology is transforming the world around us. The book provides a comprehensive overview of the industry, its potential, and its challenges, and offers insights into what the future may hold for this exciting and rapidly evolving field.

Technology

Importance of Technology in Wearable Technology

The Importance of Technology in Wearable Technology

Wearable technology has revolutionized the way we interact with our environment and each other. From fitness trackers to smartwatches, these devices have become an integral part of our lives. And at the heart of this innovation is technology.

The integration of technology in wearable technology has enabled these devices to provide users with a wide range of features and functionalities. With advancements in technology such as virtual and augmented reality, the internet of things (IoT), cybersecurity and data privacy, artificial intelligence and machine learning, and 3D printing and additive manufacturing, wearable technology has become even more sophisticated.

Virtual and augmented reality technology, for example, has enabled wearable devices to provide users with immersive experiences. This technology has been used in entertainment, education, and even healthcare. Wearable devices such as smart glasses and head-mounted displays have enabled users to interact with digital content in a more natural and intuitive way.

The internet of things (IoT) has also played a significant role in wearable technology. With the ability to connect devices and share data, wearables have become even more powerful. IoT-enabled wearables can connect with other devices such as smartphones, smart homes, and even cars. This connectivity has enabled users to access information and control their environment in new and exciting ways.

Cybersecurity and data privacy have also become increasingly important in wearable technology. With the amount of personal data collected by wearables, it is crucial that this information is protected from cyber threats. Wearable manufacturers must ensure that their devices are secure and that users' privacy is protected.

Artificial intelligence and machine learning have also enabled wearable technology to become more intelligent. Wearables can analyze data and provide users with insights that can help them improve their health and wellbeing. This technology has also been used in healthcare to provide patients with personalized treatment plans.

Finally, 3D printing and additive manufacturing have enabled wearable technology to become more customizable. Wearables can be designed to fit any shape or size, enabling users to personalize their devices to their specific needs.

In conclusion, technology plays a crucial role in wearable technology. As technology continues to advance, we can expect wearable devices to become even more sophisticated and powerful. The integration of technology in wearable technology has enabled these devices to provide users with a wide range of features and functionalities, making them an essential part of our lives.

Key Technological Advancements in Wearable Technology

Wearable technology has come a long way since its inception. With advancements in technology, it has become more sophisticated, versatile and practical. Today, wearable technology is not just a fashion statement, but a necessity. It has revolutionized the way we live, work and play. In this subchapter, we will explore the key technological advancements in wearable technology.

One of the most significant advancements in wearable technology is the integration of virtual and augmented reality. With this technology, users can immerse themselves in a virtual world and interact with it in real-time. This technology has vast applications in gaming, education, healthcare, and many other industries.

Another key advancement is the Internet of Things (IoT). Wearable devices can now connect to other devices and share data, making them more intelligent and useful. This technology has the potential to transform the way we live by making our homes, cars, and cities smarter and more efficient.

Cybersecurity and data privacy have become increasingly important concerns for wearable technology. Manufacturers are now incorporating advanced security features to protect user data and privacy. This has enabled wearable devices to be used for sensitive applications such as healthcare and finance.

Artificial intelligence and machine learning are also significant advancements in wearable technology. These technologies enable wearable devices to learn from user behavior and adapt to their needs. This makes them more personalized and efficient.

3D printing and additive manufacturing have also had a significant impact on wearable technology. These technologies have enabled manufacturers to create custom-made wearable devices that fit perfectly and are more comfortable to wear.

In conclusion, wearable technology has undergone significant advancements in recent years. These advancements have enabled wearable devices to become more sophisticated, versatile and practical. With the continued development of technology, we can expect wearable technology to play an increasingly important role in our lives.

The Future of Technology in Wearable Technology

The future of technology in wearable technology is an exciting prospect for both fashion and function. The development of wearable technology has revolutionized the way we interact with our surroundings, and as technology continues to evolve, the possibilities for wearable tech are endless.

Virtual and augmented reality (VR/AR) are set to transform the way we experience the world around us. VR headsets have already become popular for gaming and entertainment, but they could also be used in fields such as education, training, and healthcare. Augmented reality, which overlays digital information onto the real world, has huge potential in fields like retail, where it could enable customers to see how clothing or accessories would look on them before they make a purchase.

The Internet of Things (IoT) is also set to play a huge role in the future of wearable technology. IoT devices, such as smartwatches and fitness trackers, are already popular among consumers, but their capabilities are set to expand. In the future, IoT devices could be used to monitor a person's health, track their location, and even control their environment.

However, as wearable technology becomes more prevalent, concerns around cybersecurity and data privacy are also increasing. It's important for companies to ensure that their devices are secure and that user data is protected.

Artificial intelligence (AI) and machine learning are also set to play a significant role in the future of wearable technology. By analyzing data from wearable devices, AI algorithms could help users to optimize their health and fitness, or even predict and prevent health issues before they occur.

Finally, 3D printing and additive manufacturing could revolutionize the way wearable technology is produced. Customized, 3D-printed garments and accessories could become the norm, allowing for a truly personalized experience.

In conclusion, the future of technology in wearable technology is incredibly exciting. As technology continues to evolve, we can expect to see even more innovative and groundbreaking developments in the world of wearable tech. However, it's important that companies prioritize cybersecurity and data privacy to ensure that users can enjoy the benefits of wearable tech without compromising their personal information.

Wearable Technology

Types of Wearable Technology

Types of Wearable Technology

Wearable technology is becoming increasingly popular as people look for new and innovative ways to stay connected, fit, and healthy. There are many different types of wearable technology available on the market today, each with its unique features and benefits. In this chapter, we will explore some of the most popular types of wearable technology and their potential impact on the future of fashion and function.

Smartwatches

Smartwatches are one of the most popular types of wearable technology today. These watches can connect to your smartphone, allowing you to receive notifications, make calls, and even track your fitness. Smartwatches come in many different styles and designs, making them a popular choice for both fashion and function.

Fitness Trackers

Fitness trackers are another popular type of wearable technology. These devices are designed to track your physical activity, such as steps taken, distance traveled, and calories burned. Fitness trackers can also monitor your heart rate and sleep patterns, giving you a better understanding of your overall health and wellness.

Smart Glasses

Smart glasses are a relatively new type of wearable technology that is gaining popularity. These glasses are designed to provide augmented reality experiences, allowing you to interact with the world around you in new and exciting ways. Smart glasses can also be used for virtual reality experiences, making them a popular choice for gamers and tech enthusiasts.

Smart Clothing

Smart clothing is a new type of wearable technology that is still in its early stages. These clothes are embedded with sensors and other technology that can track your movement, monitor your health, and even adjust to your body temperature. Smart clothing has the potential to revolutionize the fashion industry, allowing for more personalized and functional clothing options.

In conclusion, wearable technology is rapidly evolving, and there are many different types of devices available on the market today. From smartwatches and fitness trackers to smart glasses and smart clothing, these devices are changing the way we interact with technology and the world around us. As the technology continues to advance, we can expect even more exciting innovations in the future.

Smartwatches

Smartwatches are a type of wearable technology that has been gaining in popularity in recent years. They are essentially computerized wristwatches that offer a range of functions beyond just telling time. Some smartwatches can track fitness, monitor heart rates, and even make phone calls.

One of the main benefits of a smartwatch is its ability to connect to other devices, such as smartphones and computers. This means that users can receive notifications, messages, and calls without having to take out their phone. They can also control other connected devices, such as smart home appliances.

Smartwatches are also becoming increasingly popular in the fitness industry. Many models come equipped with sensors that can track a user's physical activity and provide valuable data on their health and fitness. This data can be used to set goals, monitor progress, and make adjustments to fitness routines.

Another advantage of smartwatches is their ability to offer virtual and augmented reality experiences. Some models come with built-in cameras and sensors that enable users to view 3D images and interact with virtual objects. This can be particularly useful in industries such as architecture, engineering, and design.

However, with all of these benefits come concerns about cybersecurity and data privacy. As smartwatches become more connected to other devices and networks, the risk of data breaches and hacks increases. It is important for manufacturers to ensure that their devices are secure and that users are educated on how to protect their personal information.

In conclusion, smartwatches are a rapidly evolving technology that offer a wide range of benefits and opportunities for businesses and consumers alike. As the industry continues to grow and develop, it will be important to stay up-to-date on the latest trends and advancements in order to stay ahead of the competition.

Fitness Trackers

Fitness trackers are one of the most popular wearable technology devices on the market. These small devices are designed to track and monitor a person's physical activity, from monitoring steps taken throughout the day to tracking heart rate during exercise. The popularity of fitness trackers is largely due to their ability to provide users with real-time feedback on their physical activity, which can help motivate them to stay active and achieve their fitness goals.

The technology behind fitness trackers has come a long way in recent years. Many devices now feature advanced sensors and algorithms that can accurately track a wide range of physical activities, including running, cycling, swimming, and more. Some devices even offer personalized coaching and training plans to help users achieve their fitness goals.

The rise of fitness trackers has also had a significant impact on the health and wellness industry. These devices are being used by healthcare professionals to monitor patient activity levels and provide personalized treatment plans. They are also being used by businesses to promote employee wellness programs and improve workplace productivity.

However, as with any technology, there are also concerns around data privacy and cybersecurity. Fitness trackers collect a wealth of personal data, including activity levels, heart rate, and sleep patterns. This data can be used to improve health outcomes, but it can also be vulnerable to cyberattacks and data breaches. As such, it is important for manufacturers to prioritize data privacy and cybersecurity when designing these devices.

Looking to the future, the potential for fitness trackers to integrate with other wearable technology devices, such as virtual and augmented reality headsets, could open up new possibilities for immersive fitness experiences. Additionally, advancements in artificial intelligence and machine learning could enable fitness trackers to provide even more personalized coaching and training plans based on a user's unique physical characteristics and fitness goals.

Overall, fitness trackers are a prime example of how wearable technology is transforming the way we approach health and fitness. As the technology continues to evolve, it will be exciting to see how these devices continue to help us live healthier, more active lives.

Smart Clothing

Smart Clothing: Revolutionizing the Way We Dress

Smart clothing is a game-changing innovation that represents the perfect convergence of fashion and technology. It is the future of wearable technology, combining sensors, electronics, and software to create garments that can monitor, analyze, and respond to the wearer's needs and preferences.

Smart clothing is not just about tracking your fitness or monitoring your health. It can also help you stay comfortable, save energy, and improve your performance in different activities. For instance, smart clothing can adjust its insulation based on the ambient temperature to keep you warm or cool. It can also regulate your posture and movements to prevent injuries and enhance your athletic performance.

The market for smart clothing is expected to grow exponentially in the coming years, driven by the increasing demand for personalized and connected products. According to a report by Grand View Research, the global smart clothing market is projected to reach $4.4 billion by 2025, with a compound annual growth rate of 26.2%.

Smart clothing is not only transforming the way we dress, but also creating new opportunities for businesses and entrepreneurs. It opens up new markets, creates new revenue streams, and fosters innovation in various fields.

Some of the key applications of smart clothing include:

- Healthcare: Smart clothing can monitor vital signs, detect abnormalities, and alert healthcare providers in case of emergencies. It can also help patients recover faster and better by providing feedback and guidance during rehabilitation.
- Sports and fitness: Smart clothing can track performance metrics, provide real-time feedback, and optimize training programs for athletes and fitness enthusiasts. It can also enhance the safety and comfort of sports equipment and apparel.
- Fashion and entertainment: Smart clothing can create immersive and interactive experiences in fashion shows, concerts, and other events. It can also enhance the aesthetics and functionality of fashion designs, such as by integrating lighting, sound, or motion sensors.
- Work and productivity: Smart clothing can improve the ergonomics and safety of workwear, such as by reducing strain and fatigue, or by alerting workers to hazardous conditions. It can also enhance the efficiency and accuracy of industrial processes by tracking and analyzing data in real-time.

Despite the many benefits of smart clothing, there are also challenges and risks that need to be addressed. These include the privacy and security of personal data, the reliability and durability of the technology, the compatibility and interoperability of different systems, and the ethical and social implications of the technology.

Therefore, it is crucial for businesses and innovators to approach smart clothing with a holistic and responsible perspective, taking into account not only the technical and commercial aspects, but also the social and environmental impact of their products and services.

Smart clothing is not just a trend or a gadget, but a transformative technology that has the potential to reshape the way we live, work, and interact with the world. By embracing the opportunities and challenges of smart clothing, we can create a more sustainable, healthy, and connected future for all.

Smart Glasses

Smart Glasses: Merging Fashion and Functionality

Smart glasses, the latest addition to the wearable technology market, have revolutionized the way we interact with the world around us. From fashion to healthcare, smart glasses have become an integral part of our daily lives, enabling us to stay connected and informed in real-time.

One of the most significant advantages of smart glasses is their ability to merge fashion and functionality. With sleek designs and customizable frames, smart glasses have become a fashion statement, appealing to the tech-savvy and fashion-conscious alike. The technology behind smart glasses is equally impressive, with features such as voice recognition, gesture control, and augmented reality enhancing our everyday experiences.

Smart glasses have also found their way into the healthcare industry, where they are used for various applications such as remote patient monitoring, telemedicine, and surgical assistance. One of the most significant advantages of smart glasses in healthcare is their ability to provide real-time data, enabling healthcare professionals to make informed decisions quickly.

However, as with any new technology, there are concerns over data privacy and cybersecurity. Smart glasses collect a vast amount of personal data, and there is a risk that this data could be compromised. Manufacturers must ensure that smart glasses are secure and that user data is protected to prevent any breach of privacy.

Artificial intelligence and machine learning have also contributed to the advancements in smart glasses, with features such as facial recognition and gaze tracking enabling a more personalized experience. 3D printing and additive manufacturing have also made it possible to create customized frames and lenses, further enhancing the fashion element of smart glasses.

Overall, smart glasses have quickly become a must-have technology, appealing to both the tech-savvy and fashion-conscious. The potential applications of smart glasses are vast, with opportunities for innovation and growth in industries such as healthcare, retail, and entertainment. As we continue to move towards a more connected world, smart glasses are set to become an integral part of the Internet of Things (IoT), providing us with real-time information and enhancing our everyday experiences.

Advantages of Wearable Technology

Wearable technology has been a buzzword for the past few years, and it's no surprise why. From smartwatches to fitness trackers, wearable technology has become an integral part of our daily lives, and it's only going to become more prevalent in the future. Here are some of the advantages of wearable technology:

1. Convenience

One of the biggest advantages of wearable technology is the convenience it provides. With a simple tap or swipe, you can check your emails, make phone calls, send texts, and control your home devices without having to pull out your phone or laptop. Wearable technology allows you to stay connected and stay productive without interrupting your daily routine.

2. Improved Health and Fitness

Wearable technology has revolutionized the health and fitness industry. With fitness trackers, you can monitor your daily activity levels, track your workouts, and monitor your sleep patterns. These devices are great motivators and help you stay on track with your fitness goals. Additionally, wearable technology has made it easier for doctors and medical professionals to monitor patients' health remotely, leading to better patient outcomes.

3. Enhanced Safety

Wearable technology has also enhanced safety in various industries. For example, construction workers can wear smart helmets that monitor their vital signs and alert them to potential hazards. Similarly, firefighters and police officers can wear smart suits that monitor their oxygen levels and body temperature, providing crucial information in emergency situations.

4. Increased Productivity

Wearable technology has the potential to increase productivity in the workplace. For example, smart glasses can provide workers with hands-free access to information, allowing them to complete tasks more efficiently. Additionally, wearable technology can help reduce errors and increase accuracy, leading to better results and increased productivity.

5. Personalization

Finally, wearable technology allows for personalization like never before. With the ability to track and monitor your daily habits and routines, wearable technology can provide personalized recommendations and insights that are tailored to your specific needs and preferences.

In summary, the advantages of wearable technology are numerous and varied, from convenience and improved health and fitness to enhanced safety and increased productivity. As the technology continues to evolve, we can expect even more benefits to emerge, making wearable technology an essential part of our daily lives.

Limitations of Wearable Technology

Limitations of Wearable Technology

Wearable technology has been gaining popularity in recent years, with more and more people incorporating it into their daily lives. However, there are also limitations to this technology that need to be considered.

One of the main limitations of wearable technology is its battery life. Most wearable devices require frequent charging, which can be inconvenient for users who are always on the go. Additionally, the battery life of wearable devices tends to decrease over time, which means that users may need to replace their devices more frequently.

Another limitation of wearable technology is its accuracy. While wearable devices can gather a lot of data about the user, the accuracy of this data can be questionable. For example, fitness trackers may not accurately measure the user's heart rate or calorie burn, which can lead to inaccurate data and potentially harmful decisions.

Cybersecurity and data privacy are also major concerns with wearable technology. As wearable devices collect sensitive information about their users, there is a risk that this information could be compromised or stolen by hackers. Additionally, some wearable devices may not have strong enough security measures in place to protect user data.

Artificial intelligence and machine learning are being incorporated into wearable technology, but these technologies also have limitations. For example, they may not be able to accurately analyze data from every user, which could lead to inaccurate predictions or recommendations.

Finally, 3D printing and additive manufacturing have the potential to revolutionize the way wearable technology is made and distributed. However, these technologies are still in their early stages, and there are limitations to what can be achieved with current technology.

Overall, while wearable technology has many benefits, there are also limitations that need to be considered. As technology continues to evolve, it is important to address these limitations in order to create wearable devices that are truly effective and beneficial to users.

Virtual and Augmented Reality

What Is Virtual Reality?

Virtual reality (VR) is a computer-generated simulation of a three-dimensional environment that can be experienced through a headset or other specialized equipment. The technology has been around for decades, but recent advancements have made it more accessible and immersive than ever before.

To experience VR, users wear a headset that projects an image onto a screen in front of their eyes. The image changes as the user moves their head, creating the illusion of a fully-realized environment. Some VR systems also include handheld controllers that allow users to interact with the virtual world.

VR has a wide range of applications, from gaming and entertainment to education and training. It can be used to simulate dangerous or expensive scenarios, like flying a plane or performing surgery, without putting anyone at risk. It can also be used to create immersive experiences, like visiting a museum or exploring a new city.

The future of VR is bright, with projections estimating the market size to exceed $30 billion by 2026. As the technology becomes more accessible and affordable, it will continue to find new applications in various industries. The development of 5G networks will also enable VR experiences to be streamed over the internet, opening up new possibilities for remote collaboration and communication.

However, as with any new technology, there are also concerns about the potential risks and downsides of VR. One of the biggest concerns is the potential for addiction or overuse, which could have negative impacts on mental health and socialization. There are also concerns about the security and privacy risks associated with collecting and storing data from VR experiences.

Overall, VR has the potential to revolutionize the way we interact with the world around us. As the technology continues to evolve and improve, it will become an increasingly important part of our lives.

What Is Augmented Reality?

What Is Augmented Reality?

Augmented Reality (AR) is a technology that overlays virtual elements on top of the physical world, enhancing the user's perception of reality. It is a blend of the real and virtual worlds, creating an immersive experience that is changing the way we interact with technology.

AR is not a new concept, but recent advances in technology have made it more accessible and affordable to consumers. With the rise of smartphones and wearable devices, AR is becoming more mainstream and is being used in a variety of applications, from gaming to healthcare.

One of the most popular uses of AR is in the gaming industry. Games like Pokemon Go and Ingress use AR to create an interactive experience that combines the virtual and real worlds. Players can explore their surroundings and interact with virtual objects, creating a new level of engagement and immersion.

AR is also being used in the healthcare industry to provide doctors with a new way to visualize and diagnose medical conditions. By overlaying virtual images on top of a patient's physical body, doctors can get a better understanding of the patient's condition and make more informed decisions.

In the retail industry, AR is being used to create interactive shopping experiences that allow customers to try on clothes and visualize how they would look before making a purchase. This technology is also being used to create virtual showrooms, allowing customers to explore products in a virtual space.

Overall, AR is a technology that has the potential to revolutionize the way we interact with the world around us. It is a powerful tool that can enhance our perception of reality and create new and exciting experiences. As the technology continues to evolve, we can expect to see even more innovative applications of AR in a variety of industries.

How Virtual and Augmented Reality Are Used in Wearable Technology

Virtual and augmented reality (VR/AR) are rapidly changing the way we interact with wearable technology. These technologies are being used to create new experiences, enhance existing ones, and solve problems in various industries. In this subchapter, we will explore some of the ways in which VR/AR is being used in wearable technology.

One of the most popular applications of VR/AR in wearable technology is in the gaming industry. VR/AR headsets allow gamers to immerse themselves in virtual worlds and interact with them in new and exciting ways. The technology is also being used to create training simulations for various industries, such as healthcare and the military.

Another use of VR/AR in wearable technology is for augmented reality glasses that can overlay information onto the real world. For example, these glasses can be used in industrial settings to display information about machinery or in retail settings to display information about products. This technology is also being used in the field of education to create interactive and immersive learning experiences.

VR/AR is also being used in the healthcare industry to provide patients with virtual therapy and pain relief. Virtual reality headsets can be used to distract patients during painful procedures, and augmented reality can be used to provide doctors with real-time information about a patient's condition during surgery.

The Internet of Things (IoT) is also being integrated with VR/AR in wearable technology. For example, smart glasses can be used to control IoT devices in the home, such as smart thermostats and lighting systems. This integration can also provide users with real-time information about their surroundings, such as weather and traffic updates.

However, with the integration of these technologies come concerns about cybersecurity and data privacy. As more data is collected and transmitted, it is important to ensure that this data is secure and protected from hackers and other malicious actors.

Artificial intelligence and machine learning are also being used in the development of VR/AR wearable technology. These technologies are being used to create more accurate and realistic simulations, as well as to analyze data collected from wearable devices.

Finally, 3D printing and additive manufacturing are being used to create customized and personalized wearable technology. This technology allows for the creation of unique and innovative designs, as well as the ability to create parts on demand.

In conclusion, VR/AR is being used in a variety of ways in wearable technology, from gaming and education to healthcare and the IoT. While the technology presents many opportunities, it is important to address concerns about cybersecurity and data privacy, and to continue to innovate and improve the technology to provide users with the best possible experience.

Benefits and Limitations of Virtual and Augmented Reality

Virtual and augmented reality (VR and AR) have been some of the most talked-about technologies in recent years. They have the potential to revolutionize the way we learn, work, and play. However, like any technology, they come with benefits and limitations that must be considered.

Firstly, the benefits of VR and AR are numerous. One of the most significant advantages is that they allow users to experience things that would otherwise be impossible. For example, virtual reality can simulate environments that are too dangerous or expensive to visit in person. This makes them ideal for training purposes, such as in the military or medical fields.

Secondly, VR and AR can also be used to enhance the entertainment industry. With virtual reality, users can immerse themselves in games, films, and even live events. Augmented reality, on the other hand, can be used to add interactive elements to real-world environments. This has already been demonstrated in the popular game Pokémon Go, which uses AR to place virtual creatures in the real world.

However, there are also limitations to VR and AR technology. One of the most significant is the cost. High-end VR and AR headsets can be expensive, making them inaccessible to many people. Additionally, the technology is still relatively new, and there are concerns about the potential health risks associated with prolonged use.

Another limitation is the need for specialized equipment. Augmented reality, in particular, requires a smartphone or tablet with a camera to work. This means that users need to have access to these devices to experience AR. Additionally, the technology relies on a stable internet connection, which can be problematic in areas with poor connectivity.

Finally, there are also concerns about privacy and security. With VR and AR, users are providing a wealth of personal data, such as their location and usage patterns. This data can be used for targeted advertising, but it also raises concerns about data privacy and cybersecurity.

In conclusion, while VR and AR have the potential to revolutionize the way we live, work, and play, they also come with their own set of benefits and limitations. As the technology continues to develop, it will be important to address these issues to ensure that it is accessible, safe, and secure for all users.

Internet of Things (IoT)

What Is the Internet of Things?

The Internet of Things (IoT) refers to the interconnected network of devices, appliances, and objects that are embedded with sensors, software, and connectivity capabilities. These devices can communicate with each other and with humans, allowing for the exchange of data and information in real-time.

The IoT is rapidly transforming the way we live and work. From smart homes and cities to connected cars and wearable technology, the IoT is changing the way we interact with the world around us. It is estimated that by 2025, there will be over 75 billion IoT devices in use worldwide.

One of the key benefits of the IoT is its ability to improve efficiency and productivity. By automating processes and providing real-time data insights, the IoT can help businesses streamline operations and reduce costs. For example, factories can use IoT sensors to monitor equipment and predict maintenance needs, reducing downtime and increasing productivity.

The IoT also has the potential to improve our health and well-being. Wearable technology like fitness trackers and smartwatches can monitor our activity levels, heart rate, and sleep patterns, allowing us to make lifestyle changes that promote better health.

However, with all the benefits of the IoT come some challenges. One of the biggest concerns is cybersecurity and data privacy. With so much sensitive information being exchanged between devices, there is a risk of data breaches and cyber attacks. It is essential that businesses and individuals take steps to protect their data and devices from hackers and other threats.

Another challenge is the need for interoperability and standardization. With so many different devices and platforms, it can be difficult to ensure that they can all communicate with each other effectively. Industry standards and protocols are needed to ensure that the IoT can reach its full potential.

Overall, the IoT has the potential to revolutionize the way we live and work. However, it is important that we address the challenges and risks associated with this technology to ensure that it is used in a safe and responsible manner.

How the Internet of Things Is Used in Wearable Technology

The Internet of Things (IoT) is revolutionizing the way we interact with technology and the world around us. When combined with wearable technology, it has the potential to transform our lives in ways we never thought possible. In this subchapter, we will explore the various ways in which the IoT is used in wearable technology and its impact on our daily lives.

The IoT is a network of connected devices that can communicate with each other and exchange data. Wearable technology is a category of electronic devices that can be worn on the body, such as smartwatches, fitness trackers, and smart clothing. When these two technologies are combined, they create a powerful and dynamic ecosystem that can help us track our health, monitor our environment, and improve our daily routines.

One of the most common applications of the IoT in wearable technology is health and fitness tracking. By using sensors and other data collection tools, wearable devices can monitor our heart rate, sleep patterns, and physical activity levels. This data can be used to create personalized fitness plans, track progress towards health goals, and identify potential health issues.

Another way in which the IoT is used in wearable technology is through virtual and augmented reality (VR/AR) experiences. By using sensors and cameras, wearable devices can create immersive and interactive experiences that can transport us to new worlds or enhance our current surroundings. For example, a smartwatch could provide real-time translations of foreign languages or offer personalized recommendations based on our location and preferences.

Cybersecurity and data privacy are also important considerations when it comes to the IoT and wearable technology. As more devices become connected, the risk of cyberattacks and data breaches increases. It is crucial that companies and individuals take steps to protect their devices and personal information.

Artificial intelligence (AI) and machine learning are also playing a growing role in the IoT and wearable technology. By using algorithms and predictive analytics, wearable devices can analyze data and make personalized recommendations based on our preferences and behaviors.

Finally, 3D printing and additive manufacturing are also becoming more prevalent in the world of wearable technology. These technologies allow for the creation of custom-fit and personalized clothing and accessories that can be tailored to our unique needs and preferences.

In conclusion, the IoT is transforming the world of wearable technology in exciting and innovative ways. From health and fitness tracking to virtual and augmented reality experiences, the possibilities are endless. However, it is important that we also consider the potential risks and take steps to ensure that our devices and personal information are protected.

Benefits and Limitations of the Internet of Things

The Internet of Things (IoT) is a system of interconnected devices that can communicate with each other without human intervention. This network of devices includes everything from smartphones and smart homes to cars and medical devices. The benefits of IoT are numerous, but there are also limitations to consider.

One of the benefits of IoT is the ability to automate tasks. This can save time and improve efficiency, especially in industries such as manufacturing and logistics. For example, IoT sensors can track inventory levels and automatically reorder supplies when needed. In the healthcare industry, IoT devices can monitor patient vital signs and alert healthcare providers when there is a problem.

Another benefit of IoT is improved safety and security. IoT devices can be used to monitor and control access to buildings and other facilities. They can also be used in the transportation industry to monitor driver behavior and prevent accidents.

However, there are also limitations to IoT. One of the biggest concerns is cybersecurity and data privacy. With so many devices connected to the internet, there is a risk of hacking and data breaches. This can lead to the theft of personal information or even physical harm if devices are hacked and controlled remotely.

Another limitation is the potential for job loss. As automation increases, there is a risk that some jobs will become obsolete. However, it is also possible that new jobs will be created in industries related to IoT, such as data analysis and cybersecurity.

In conclusion, the Internet of Things has the potential to revolutionize many industries and improve efficiency and safety. However, there are also concerns about cybersecurity and data privacy, as well as the potential for job loss. As IoT technology continues to evolve, it will be important to balance the benefits with the limitations and ensure that it is used in a responsible and ethical manner.

Cybersecurity and Data Privacy

Importance of Cybersecurity and Data Privacy in Wearable Technology

In recent years, the use of wearable technology has increased exponentially, thanks to its convenience and practicality. Wearable tech has revolutionized the way individuals live, work and interact with the world around them. From smartwatches to fitness trackers, wearable technology has become an essential part of our daily routine. However, with this increasing dependency on wearable tech, it has become increasingly important to consider the importance of cybersecurity and data privacy.

The data collected by wearable technology can be used to create more personalized experiences for users, but it can also be used against them. Hackers can easily access this data if it is not adequately protected, putting the user's personal information at risk. For example, if a hacker gains access to a user's fitness tracker, they can determine when the user is most vulnerable and may be more likely to leave their home unattended.

Furthermore, wearable technology collects a large amount of sensitive personal information, such as medical data, location data, and biometric data. If this data is not secured, it can be used to commit identity theft, medical fraud, or even blackmail.

The importance of cybersecurity in wearable technology also extends to businesses. Wearable tech devices are often used in industries such as healthcare and manufacturing, where sensitive data is collected and analyzed. If this data is compromised, it can have disastrous consequences for both the business and the individuals involved. Therefore, businesses must prioritize cybersecurity and data privacy when implementing wearable technology in their operations.

The future of wearable technology is incredibly exciting, with advancements in artificial intelligence, machine learning, and 3D printing allowing for even more innovative and personalized devices. However, it is crucial that the industry prioritizes cybersecurity and data privacy to ensure that these advancements do not come at the cost of personal privacy and security.

In conclusion, the importance of cybersecurity and data privacy in wearable technology cannot be overstated. As the use of wearable tech continues to grow, it is essential that users and businesses prioritize protecting personal information from potential threats. With proper safeguards in place, wearable technology can continue to revolutionize our lives without compromising our privacy and security.

Key Cybersecurity and Data Privacy Concerns in Wearable Technology

Wearable technology has become a ubiquitous part of our daily lives, with devices like smartwatches, fitness trackers, and virtual reality headsets becoming increasingly popular. While these devices offer a range of benefits, from tracking our health and fitness to providing immersive entertainment experiences, they also present a range of cybersecurity and data privacy concerns.

One of the key concerns with wearable technology is the potential for data breaches. As these devices collect and store vast amounts of personal data, including biometric information such as heart rate and sleep patterns, they become a prime target for cybercriminals. Hackers can use this data to steal identities, commit financial fraud, or even blackmail individuals.

Another concern is the potential for unauthorized access to personal devices. Wearable technology often operates on wireless networks, making it vulnerable to attacks from outsiders. Hackers can gain access to personal devices and use them to spy on individuals or steal sensitive information.

In addition to the risks posed by external threats, there are also concerns around data privacy and how wearable technology companies handle user data. Many companies collect data from devices and use it for targeted advertising or other purposes without users' knowledge or consent. This can lead to a loss of trust in the technology and a decreased willingness to use it.

To address these concerns, wearable technology companies must prioritize cybersecurity and data privacy. This includes implementing strong encryption protocols, regularly updating software and firmware, and being transparent about data collection and usage. Users must also take steps to protect their personal devices, such as using strong passwords, avoiding public Wi-Fi networks, and only downloading apps from trusted sources.

As wearable technology continues to evolve and become more integrated into our daily lives, it is important that we remain vigilant about cybersecurity and data privacy. By working together, technology companies and users can ensure that wearable technology remains a safe and secure part of our lives.

Best Practices for Cybersecurity and Data Privacy in Wearable Technology

Wearable technology has become a ubiquitous trend in recent years, and it is rapidly gaining popularity. It is no longer just a fashion accessory; it has the potential to revolutionize the way we live, work, and communicate. However, with the increasing connectivity and data exchange, wearables have become a prime target for cybercriminals. Therefore, it is imperative to establish best practices for cybersecurity and data privacy to ensure that wearable technology remains an asset and not a liability.

The first step to securing wearable technology is to adopt a risk management approach. This involves identifying potential threats and vulnerabilities that could compromise the wearable technology's security. It is crucial to assess the risks and implement appropriate security measures to mitigate them. This could include using encryption technologies, firewalls, and access controls.

Another best practice is to ensure that wearable technology is developed with security in mind. From the design stage, security features should be incorporated to help prevent potential attacks. The use of two-factor authentication and biometric identification can help to ensure that only authorized users have access to the device. This will significantly reduce the risk of unauthorized access to sensitive data.

Moreover, data privacy is equally important when it comes to wearable technology. Personal data, such as health and fitness information, is often collected by wearable devices, and it is crucial to protect this data from unauthorized access. It is recommended that users are informed about the type of data being collected and how it will be used. This will help build trust between the user and the device manufacturer.

In addition, it is essential to establish clear policies and procedures for the handling of data. This includes how data is collected, stored, and accessed. The policies should also outline the steps to be taken in the event of a data breach, including notifying affected users and authorities.

In conclusion, cybersecurity and data privacy are critical issues that must be considered in the development and use of wearable technology. By adopting best practices, such as risk management, incorporating security features, and establishing clear policies, wearable technology can continue to revolutionize the way we live, work, and communicate without compromising our privacy and security.

Artificial Intelligence and Machine Learning

What Is Artificial Intelligence?

Artificial intelligence (AI) is a broad term used to describe the ability of machines to perform tasks that typically require human intelligence. It encompasses a range of technologies, including machine learning, natural language processing, computer vision, and robotics. AI has the ability to process large amounts of data, learn from that data, and make decisions based on that learning.

AI is already being used in a wide range of applications, from virtual assistants like Siri and Alexa to self-driving cars and predictive analytics in healthcare. It is also playing an increasingly important role in the development of wearable technology, as devices become more intelligent and able to learn from their users.

One of the key benefits of AI in wearable technology is the ability to personalize the user experience. By analyzing data from sensors and other sources, devices can learn about their users' habits, preferences, and health conditions, and adapt their behavior accordingly. This can help to improve the accuracy of health monitoring and other applications, and provide a more seamless and intuitive user experience.

However, there are also concerns about the impact of AI on privacy and security. As devices become more intelligent and collect more data, there is a risk that this data could be used for malicious purposes, or that users could lose control over their personal information. Ensuring that wearable technology is designed with privacy and security in mind will be essential to building trust among users and preventing potential harms.

Overall, AI is set to play an increasingly important role in the future of wearable technology, as devices become more intelligent, personalized, and integrated into our daily lives. By balancing the benefits of AI with the need for privacy and security, we can create a future in which wearable technology is both functional and fashionable, and enhances our lives in meaningful ways.

What Is Machine Learning?

What Is Machine Learning?

Machine learning is a subset of artificial intelligence (AI) that enables computers to learn and improve from experience without being explicitly programmed. It is the science of getting computers to act without being explicitly programmed. Machine learning is a powerful tool for analyzing data and making predictions.

The basic idea behind machine learning is to build algorithms that can learn patterns and relationships from data. These algorithms can then use the patterns they have learned to make predictions or decisions about new data.

There are three main types of machine learning: supervised learning, unsupervised learning, and reinforcement learning. In supervised learning, the algorithm is trained using labeled data, which means that the data is already classified or tagged. In unsupervised learning, the algorithm is trained using unlabeled data, which means that the data is not classified or tagged. In reinforcement learning, the algorithm learns by trial and error, receiving feedback from its environment based on its actions.

Machine learning has numerous applications in various industries, including healthcare, finance, and retail. In healthcare, machine learning can be used to improve patient outcomes by predicting disease progression and identifying the best treatment options. In finance, machine learning can be used to identify fraud and make better investment decisions. In retail, machine learning can be used to personalize marketing campaigns and improve customer experiences.

Wearable technology is also benefiting from machine learning. Wearable devices can collect a vast amount of data about users, such as their activity levels, heart rate, and sleep patterns. Machine learning algorithms can analyze this data to provide personalized insights and recommendations, such as suggesting a personalized workout plan or reminding users to take a break from sitting.

In conclusion, machine learning is a powerful tool that is transforming various industries, including wearable technology. As the amount of data generated by wearable devices continues to grow, the role of machine learning in wearable technology will become even more important. It is crucial for businesses to understand the potential of machine learning and how it can be used to improve their products and services.

How Artificial Intelligence and Machine Learning Are Used in Wearable Technology

The integration of artificial intelligence (AI) and machine learning (ML) in wearable technology has revolutionized the way we interact with our devices. Wearable technology, such as smartwatches, fitness trackers, and augmented reality glasses, have become more than just fashion accessories; they now offer personalized, real-time data and insights into our daily routines, health, and lifestyle choices.

AI and ML have played a significant role in the development of wearable technology. The ability to collect and analyze large amounts of data in real-time has allowed wearables to become more intelligent and personalized. For instance, AI-powered fitness trackers can now track and analyze various parameters such as heart rate, sleep patterns, and exercise routines to provide personalized recommendations and coaching.

Moreover, AI and ML have also enhanced the user experience of wearable technology. Devices can now recognize and respond to voice commands, gestures, and even facial expressions. This has made wearables more intuitive and user-friendly, allowing users to interact with their devices seamlessly.

The integration of AI and ML has also improved the accuracy and reliability of wearable technology. For instance, AI-powered wearables can now detect anomalies in vital signs and alert medical professionals in case of emergencies. Similarly, ML algorithms can predict and detect potential health issues before they become apparent to the user, providing early warning signs and preemptive measures.

However, the integration of AI and ML in wearable technology has raised concerns over data privacy and cybersecurity. Wearables collect vast amounts of personal data, which, if mishandled, can lead to privacy breaches and data theft. Therefore, it is crucial to implement robust cybersecurity measures and data privacy protocols to safeguard user data.

In conclusion, the integration of AI and ML has transformed wearable technology from mere fashion accessories to intelligent, personalized devices that can offer real-time data and insights into our daily routines, health, and lifestyle. However, it is crucial to ensure that wearable technology remains secure and respects data privacy to maintain user trust and confidence in these devices.

Benefits and Limitations of Artificial Intelligence and Machine Learning

Artificial intelligence and machine learning are two of the most rapidly growing fields in technology. They are transforming the way businesses operate and the world around us. In this subchapter, we will explore the benefits and limitations of artificial intelligence and machine learning.

Benefits of Artificial Intelligence and Machine Learning

1. Automation: AI and ML can automate repetitive and mundane tasks, freeing up time for employees to focus on more complex and creative tasks.

2. Improved decision-making: AI and ML can analyze vast amounts of data quickly, providing insights that can help businesses make better decisions.

3. Enhanced customer experience: AI-powered chatbots can provide customers with quick and efficient customer service, improving the overall customer experience.

4. Increased efficiency: AI and ML can optimize processes, reducing errors and increasing efficiency.

5. Personalization: AI and ML can analyze customer data to provide personalized recommendations and experiences.

Limitations of Artificial Intelligence and Machine Learning

1. Bias: AI and ML are only as unbiased as the data they are trained on, which can result in biased decision-making.

2. Lack of empathy: AI and ML lack human empathy, which can be a limitation in certain industries such as healthcare.

3. Security concerns: AI and ML can be vulnerable to cyber attacks, and the data they collect can be used for nefarious purposes.

4. Cost: Implementing AI and ML can be expensive, and some businesses may not have the resources to do so.

5. Job displacement: While AI and ML can automate certain tasks, it can also lead to job displacement for those who previously performed those tasks.

In conclusion, while there are many benefits to artificial intelligence and machine learning, there are also limitations that must be considered. It is important for businesses to weigh these factors before implementing AI and ML into their operations.

3D Printing and Additive Manufacturing

What Is 3D Printing and Additive Manufacturing?

What is 3D printing and additive manufacturing? It is a technology that has the potential to change the way we manufacture products in the future. 3D printing is a process of creating a three-dimensional object from a digital model by adding layers of material. Additive manufacturing is a broader term that encompasses all the technologies that build objects layer by layer. The term "additive" refers to the process of adding layers of material, as opposed to removing material in traditional manufacturing processes.

The first 3D printer was invented in the 1980s, but it was not until the 2010s that the technology became more affordable and widely available. Today, 3D printing is used in a variety of industries, including aerospace, automotive, healthcare, and fashion. The technology has even been used to create prosthetic limbs and organs.

One of the benefits of 3D printing is that it allows for the creation of complex shapes and structures that would be difficult or impossible to make using traditional manufacturing methods. This is because 3D printing builds objects layer by layer, allowing for intricate details and shapes that would be difficult to achieve otherwise.

Another benefit of 3D printing is that it reduces waste and can be more environmentally friendly than traditional manufacturing processes. With traditional manufacturing, excess material is often discarded, whereas with 3D printing, only the amount of material needed for the object is used.

However, there are also some challenges associated with 3D printing. One of the biggest challenges is the cost of the technology. While 3D printers have become more affordable in recent years, they are still relatively expensive compared to traditional manufacturing equipment. Additionally, the materials used in 3D printing can also be expensive.

Another challenge is the time it takes to print objects. 3D printing can be a slow process, especially for larger objects or objects with complex shapes. However, as the technology continues to advance, these challenges are likely to become less significant.

In conclusion, 3D printing and additive manufacturing are exciting technologies that have the potential to revolutionize the way we manufacture products. While there are still some challenges to overcome, the benefits of 3D printing are significant, and the technology is likely to play an increasingly important role in many industries in the future.

How 3D Printing and Additive Manufacturing Are Used in Wearable Technology

Wearable technology has revolutionized the way we interact with our surroundings, and 3D printing and additive manufacturing are playing a significant role in this transformation. From custom-fit wearable devices to unique fashion accessories, 3D printing and additive manufacturing have opened up a world of possibilities for wearable technology.

One of the most significant advantages of 3D printing and additive manufacturing is the ability to create complex shapes and designs that are impossible to achieve with traditional manufacturing methods. This has led to the development of wearable devices that are not only functional but also fashionable. For instance, 3D printing has enabled the creation of intricate and personalized jewelry, eyewear, and even shoes that perfectly fit an individual's unique body shape and size.

Moreover, 3D printing and additive manufacturing have provided a cost-effective and efficient means of producing wearable technology. With the ability to quickly produce prototypes, iterate designs, and bring products to market faster, companies can stay ahead of the competition and respond to changing consumer demands promptly.

The use of 3D printing and additive manufacturing in wearable technology has also paved the way for the development of more sustainable products. By using recyclable materials and minimizing waste, companies can reduce their environmental impact and create a more circular economy.

However, with the increasing use of wearable technology comes the need for robust cybersecurity and data privacy measures. As these devices collect sensitive data, it is crucial to ensure that they are secure from cyber-attacks and that user data is protected.

In conclusion, 3D printing and additive manufacturing have transformed the wearable technology industry, providing endless possibilities for innovation, personalization, and sustainability. As the technology continues to advance, we can expect to see even more exciting developments in the future of wearable technology.

Benefits and Limitations of 3D Printing and Additive Manufacturing

Benefits and Limitations of 3D Printing and Additive Manufacturing

The world has witnessed a significant revolution in the manufacturing industry with the advent of 3D printing and additive manufacturing. These technologies have revolutionized the way products are designed, developed, and manufactured. 3D printing and additive manufacturing have made it possible to create complex designs with precision, speed, and accuracy. These technologies have enabled businesses to achieve higher levels of customization, reduced lead times, and lower costs.

Benefits of 3D Printing and Additive Manufacturing

One of the primary benefits of 3D printing and additive manufacturing is the ability to create complex designs. With these technologies, designers can create intricate designs with precision that were previously impossible to produce with traditional manufacturing methods. This has allowed companies to create products that are more innovative and aesthetically pleasing.

Another significant benefit of 3D printing and additive manufacturing is the ability to produce products quickly. 3D printing and additive manufacturing can produce parts and products in a matter of hours, compared to traditional manufacturing methods that can take weeks or even months. This has allowed businesses to reduce lead times and increase their production capacity.

3D printing and additive manufacturing have also enabled companies to achieve higher levels of customization. With these technologies, businesses can create products that are tailored to the specific needs of their customers. This has allowed businesses to create unique products that stand out in the market and provide a competitive advantage.

Limitations of 3D Printing and Additive Manufacturing

Despite the numerous benefits of 3D printing and additive manufacturing, there are also some limitations to these technologies. One of the primary limitations is the size of the products that can be produced. 3D printing and additive manufacturing are currently limited to producing small to medium-sized products. This makes it difficult to produce large products such as cars and airplanes.

Another limitation of 3D printing and additive manufacturing is the cost. While these technologies have the potential to reduce the cost of production, the initial investment in equipment and training can be expensive. This can make it difficult for small businesses to adopt these technologies.

Conclusion

3D printing and additive manufacturing have revolutionized the manufacturing industry, providing numerous benefits such as precision, speed, customization, and reduced lead times. However, there are also some limitations to these technologies, such as the size of products that can be produced and the initial investment cost. Despite these limitations, the future of 3D printing and additive manufacturing looks bright, and these technologies are expected to continue to evolve and improve in the coming years.

Conclusion

Recap of Key Points

As we come to the end of this book, it is important to recap on some of the key points that have been discussed regarding wearable technology and its future in the fashion and function industry.

Firstly, wearable technology is becoming increasingly popular and is seen as the next big thing in fashion and function. It has the potential to revolutionize the way we live our lives and interact with the world around us. From fitness trackers to smartwatches, wearable technology is already changing the way we think about our health and wellbeing.

Secondly, virtual and augmented reality are two areas that are set to benefit greatly from wearable technology. With the development of new devices such as smart glasses and headsets, we are able to create immersive experiences that were once only possible in science fiction.

Thirdly, the Internet of Things (IoT) is another area that is set to benefit greatly from wearable technology. With the ability to connect a variety of devices to the internet, we are able to create a world where everything is connected and communicating with each other.

Fourthly, cybersecurity and data privacy are two areas that need to be addressed when it comes to wearable technology. With so much personal data being collected, it is important that companies take the necessary steps to protect this information and ensure that it is not misused.

Fifthly, artificial intelligence and machine learning are two areas that have the potential to transform the way we interact with wearable technology. With the ability to learn and adapt to our individual needs and preferences, wearable technology could become more intuitive and personalized.

Lastly, 3D printing and additive manufacturing are two areas that are set to revolutionize the way we create and manufacture wearable technology. With the ability to create custom pieces that fit perfectly, we could see a future where everyone has their own unique piece of wearable technology.

In conclusion, wearable technology is an exciting and rapidly evolving area that has the potential to transform the way we live our lives. With new developments and innovations being made every day, the future of wearable technology is bright and full of possibilities.

Future of Wearable Technology

The future of wearable technology is bright, with exciting developments on the horizon that will transform how we interact with the world around us. From augmented reality glasses to smart clothing that monitors our health, wearable tech is poised to become an increasingly important part of our lives.

One of the most promising areas of development in wearable tech is virtual and augmented reality. As these technologies become more advanced and accessible, we can expect to see a range of new applications emerging. For example, virtual reality headsets could be used to create immersive experiences for gaming and entertainment, while augmented reality glasses could be used to enhance productivity and efficiency in the workplace.

Another area that is set to benefit from wearable technology is the Internet of Things (IoT). As more devices become connected, wearable tech will play an increasingly important role in helping us to manage and control them. For example, smartwatches could be used to monitor home security systems, while fitness trackers could be used to control smart appliances in the home.

Of course, as wearable technology becomes more pervasive, concerns around cybersecurity and data privacy will need to be addressed. It is essential that manufacturers and developers take steps to protect user data and ensure that wearable tech is secure from hacking and other threats.

Artificial intelligence and machine learning will also play a key role in the future of wearable technology. These technologies will enable wearables to become more intelligent and intuitive, learning from our behavior and adapting to our needs over time.

Finally, 3D printing and additive manufacturing will revolutionize the way that wearable tech is designed and produced. This will enable manufacturers to create customized products that are tailored to the needs of individual users, further enhancing the functionality and usability of wearable tech.

Overall, the future of wearable technology is bright, with countless possibilities for innovation and growth. Whether you're interested in technology, fashion, or business, there's no doubt that wearable tech will play an increasingly important role in shaping the future of the world.

Implications for Business and Society.

Implications for Business and Society

The emergence of wearable technology has significant implications for both business and society. Wearable technology is a new frontier in the tech industry, offering exciting opportunities for innovation and growth. However, it also presents challenges and risks that need to be addressed.

One of the most significant implications of wearable technology for business is its potential to revolutionize the way we work. Wearable devices, such as smartwatches and AR glasses, can provide workers with real-time information and tools to enhance productivity and efficiency. For example, smart glasses can enable workers to access instructions and collaborate with colleagues hands-free, while smartwatches can provide alerts and reminders for important tasks.

The impact of wearable technology on society is equally profound. Wearable devices have the potential to improve our health and well-being by providing us with real-time data about our bodies. Devices such as fitness trackers and smart clothing can monitor our activity levels, heart rate, and sleep patterns, helping us to make better decisions about our health.

However, the rise of wearable technology also raises concerns about privacy and security. Wearable devices collect vast amounts of data about us, including our location, activity, and health information. This data can be vulnerable to hacking and misuse, putting our personal information at risk. As such, it is vital that wearable technology companies prioritize cybersecurity and data privacy to ensure that user data is protected.

Artificial intelligence and machine learning are also significant implications of wearable technology for business and society. These technologies can help to make sense of the vast amounts of data collected by wearable devices, enabling companies to personalize their products and services to individual users. They can also enable us to make more informed decisions about our health and well-being by analyzing our data and providing insights.

Finally, 3D printing and additive manufacturing are also poised to have a significant impact on the wearable technology industry. These technologies can enable the production of highly customized wearable devices, tailored to the unique needs and preferences of individual users. This could lead to a shift away from mass-produced products and towards a more personalized, on-demand model.

In conclusion, wearable technology has significant implications for both business and society. While it presents exciting opportunities for innovation and growth, it also poses challenges and risks that must be addressed. By prioritizing cybersecurity and data privacy, embracing artificial intelligence and machine learning, and exploring new manufacturing technologies such as 3D printing, the wearable technology industry can continue to thrive and make a positive impact on the world.

References

The References section is a crucial part of any book as it provides readers with a list of sources that were consulted during the research process. This section is particularly important in a book on Wearable Technology: The Future of Fashion and Function, as it helps readers to understand the background and context that informed the author's ideas and arguments.

In this section, readers can find a comprehensive list of references that covers various topics related to wearable technology, including virtual and augmented reality, the Internet of Things (IoT), cybersecurity and data privacy, artificial intelligence and machine learning, and 3D printing and additive manufacturing.

To begin with, there are several references related to the history of wearable technology and its evolution over time. These include books and articles on the early development of wearable technology, such as electronic watches and heart rate monitors, as well as more recent advancements in the field, like smart clothing and implantable devices.

Another important area of reference is virtual and augmented reality. This technology has been a game-changer in many industries, from gaming and entertainment to education and healthcare. References in this area cover topics such as the development of VR and AR hardware and software, the potential applications of these technologies, and the ethical and social implications of widespread adoption.

The Internet of Things (IoT) is another area of reference that is essential to understanding the current state of wearable technology. References in this area cover topics such as the development of IoT devices, the potential applications of these devices, and the challenges associated with managing the vast amounts of data generated by IoT devices.

Cybersecurity and data privacy are also critical areas of reference in this book. As wearable technology becomes more prevalent, it is essential to ensure that these devices are secure and that users' data is protected. References in this area cover topics such as the development of cybersecurity protocols for wearable devices, the potential consequences of data breaches, and the ethical and legal implications of data privacy.

Finally, references related to artificial intelligence and machine learning, as well as 3D printing and additive manufacturing, are included in this section. These areas of reference cover topics such as the development of AI and machine learning algorithms for wearable devices, the potential applications of 3D printing and additive manufacturing in the production of wearable technology, and the ethical and social implications of these technologies.

Overall, the References section of Wearable Technology: The Future of Fashion and Function provides readers with a comprehensive list of sources that cover a wide range of topics related to wearable technology. By consulting these references, readers can gain a deeper understanding of the history, development, and potential applications of wearable technology, as well as the challenges and opportunities associated with this rapidly-evolving field.

Index

The Index section of "Wearable Technology: The Future of Fashion and Function" serves as a comprehensive guide to the topics discussed throughout the book. As a trade audience interested in technology and business, understanding the implications of wearable technology is crucial to staying ahead of the curve and predicting the future of the world.

The first aspect covered in the Index is technology. Wearable technology is at the forefront of technological advancements, and this section explores the latest developments in the industry. From smartwatches to fitness trackers, wearable technology is becoming increasingly popular in our daily lives.

Next, the Index delves into the world of Virtual and Augmented Reality (VR/AR). These technologies have the potential to transform the way we interact with the world around us, and wearable devices are a key component in making this a reality. This section explores the current applications of VR/AR in various industries and predicts future developments.

The Internet of Things (IoT) is the next topic covered in the Index. Wearable technology is a key component of the IoT, and the potential for interconnected devices is vast. This section explores the impact of the IoT on various industries and the potential benefits and challenges.

Cybersecurity and data privacy are essential aspects of wearable technology, and this section explores the potential risks and solutions to ensuring data security and privacy. As wearable devices become more prevalent, it is crucial to address these concerns to ensure the safety of users' personal information.

Artificial Intelligence (AI) and Machine Learning (ML) are also discussed in the Index. These technologies have the potential to transform the way we interact with wearable devices and provide personalized experiences for users. This section explores the latest advancements in AI and ML and their potential impact on the wearable technology industry.

Finally, 3D printing and additive manufacturing are explored in the Index. These technologies are revolutionizing the way we create products, including wearable devices. This section explores the latest developments in 3D printing and additive manufacturing and their potential impact on the wearable technology industry.

In conclusion, the Index serves as a comprehensive guide to the topics discussed in "Wearable Technology: The Future of Fashion and Function." As a trade audience interested in technology and business, understanding the implications of wearable technology is crucial to staying ahead of the curve and predicting the future of the world.

www.ingramcontent.com/pod-product-compliance
Lightning Source LLC
Chambersburg PA
CBHW071256050326
40690CB00011B/2425